I0422122

The month of December, from the illuminated manuscript *Les Très Riches Heures du duc de Berry*

The Story of a Special Day
Volume 344

December

9

343rd day of the year
(344th in leap years)
22 days remaining
until the end of the year.

by Michael Dobson

Timespinner Press

Table of Contents

December 9 Quotations 3

Event of the Day 5

December 9 Holidays and Celebrations 11

What Happened on December 9? 15

Who Was Born on December 9? 25

Who Died on December 9? 53

December: The Twelfth Month 65

December Events 69

December 9 Zodiac Signs 73

What Day of the Week is December 9? 77

Copyright, Credit, and Contact 79

Cover: "The Charge of the Light Brigade" by Richard Caton Woodville, Jr., for the *Event of the Day.*

Back Cover and Frontispiece: The month of December, from the French Gothic illuminated manuscript *Les Très Riches Heures du duc de Berry.*

Redd Foxx

December 9 Quotations

"If you can see the handwriting on the wall…you're on the toilet."

> — *Redd Foxx, comedian, born December 9, 1922*

"All politics is local."

> — *Tip O'Neill, Speaker of the US House of Representatives, born December 9, 1912*

"A ship in port is safe; but that is not what ships are built for. Sail out to sea and do new things."

> — *Grace Hopper, US Navy admiral and early computer programmer, born December 9, 1906*

"Sex and laughter do go very well together, and I wondered — and still do — which is more important."

> — *Hermione Gingold, actress, born December 9, 1897*

"I'm not concerned with body building; I'm just trying to make people normal human beings."

> — *Joseph Pilates, developer of Pilates, born December 9, 1883*

"'I don't keer w'at you do wid me, Brer Fox,' sezee, 'so you don't fling me in dat brier-patch. Roas' me, Brer Fox' sezee, 'but don't fling me in dat brier-patch,' sezee."

> — *Joel Chandler Harris, author, born December 9, 1848*

"Idlers do not make history: they suffer it!"

> — *Peter Kropotkin (Пётр Кропо́ткин), scientist and anarchist, born December 9, 1842*

"They also serve who only stand and wait."

> — *John Milton, poet, born December 9, 1608*

"Remember, the inevitable inefficiency of a huge bureaucracy will be working for you."

> — *Robert Sheckley, science fiction writer, died December 9, 2005*

"Right is right if nobody is right, and wrong is wrong if everybody is wrong."

> — *Fulton J. Sheen, Roman Catholic archbishop and television preacher, died December 9, 1979*

"Hearts are strongest when they beat in response to noble ideals."

> — *Ralph Bunche, diplomat and Nobel laureate, died December 9, 1971*

"The public will believe anything, so long as it is not founded on the truth."

> — *Edith Sitwell, poet, died December 9, 1964*

Event of the Day
The Charge of the Light Brigade Published

On December 9, 1854, the weekly London newspaper *The Examiner* published a poem by Great Britain's Poet Laureate, Alfred, Lord Tennyson: *The Charge of the Light Brigade*. Famous for such lines as "Into the valley of Death / Rode the six hundred," the poem — which Tennyson wrote in just a few minutes after reading a newspaper account of the Charge — became hugely popular, and remains one of the great classics of English literature. The poem's hoofbeat cadence and patriotic tone contrast strongly with his unflinching portrayal of the horrors of war.

The actual Charge of the Light Brigade occurred on October 25, 1854, during the Battle of Balaclava, an attempt by combined English, French, and Turkish forces during the Crimean War to besiege the strategically vital Russian port of Sevastopol, located on the Black Sea. The British forces, commanded by Field Marshal the Right Honorable Lord Raglan, were responsible for the right flank of the siege, and occupied the nearby port of Balaclava with a force of about 4,500.

Alfred, Lord Tennyson (Photo: Julia Margaret Cameron)

The Charge of the Light Brigade

Alfred, Lord Tennyson

I

Half a league, half a league,
Half a league onward,
All in the valley of Death
Rode the six hundred.
"Forward, the Light Brigade!
Charge for the guns!" he said.
Into the valley of Death
Rode the six hundred.

II

"Forward, the Light Brigade!"
Was there a man dismayed?
Not though the soldier knew
Someone had blundered.
Theirs not to make reply,
Theirs not to reason why,
Theirs but to do and die.
Into the valley of Death
Rode the six hundred.

III

Cannon to right of them,
Cannon to left of them,
Cannon in front of them
Volleyed and thundered;
Stormed at with shot and
shell,
Boldly they rode and well,
Into the jaws of Death,
Into the mouth of hell
Rode the six hundred.

IV

Flashed all their sabres bare,
Flashed as they turned in air
Sabring the gunners there,
Charging an army, while
All the world wondered.
Plunged in the battery-smoke
Right through the line they
broke;
Cossack and Russian
Reeled from the sabre stroke
Shattered and sundered.
Then they rode back, but not
Not the six hundred.

V

Cannon to right of them,
Cannon to left of them,
Cannon behind them
Volleyed and thundered;
Stormed at with shot and
shell,
While horse and hero fell.
They that had fought so well
Came through the jaws of
Death,
Back from the mouth of hell,
All that was left of them,
Left of six hundred.

VI

When can their glory fade?
O the wild charge they made!
All the world wondered.
Honour the charge they made!
Honour the Light Brigade,
Noble six hundred!

Seeing the small British garrison as vulnerable, a Russian force of some 25,000 soldiers under the command of General Pavel Liprandi (Павел Петрович Липранди) attacked, but were held back by the Scottish 93rd (Highland) Regiment, which became known as the "Thin Red Line." A charge by British heavy cavalry (partially armored) pushed the Russians onto defense.

At that point, Lord Raglan decided to send his fast-moving and unarmored light cavalry, consisting of about 670 horse soldiers, in pursuit of a retreating Russian artillery battery, a role for which light cavalry are well suited. However, the orders (admittedly vague) were misinterpreted as they moved down the chain of command, and instead of being sent after the retreating battery, the Light Brigade was ordered instead to make a direct frontal assault on a *different* artillery battery, one that was well prepared and fully dug in.

The reasons for this error are still debated. Besides ambiguity in Raglan's original order, there is the possible role of he man who conveyed the order from Raglan, Captain Louis Nolan. Nolan was killed early in the charge, possibly after realizing the mistake and trying to stop it. Another possibility is the conflict between the overall cavalry commander, the Earl of Lucan, and the Light Brigade commander, Lord Cardigan (after whom the cardigan sweater is named). The two men were brothers in law who hated each other.

Finally, there was Lord Cardigan himself, a man known for arrogance and incompetence (one of his commanding officers had once called him "constitutionally unfit for command").

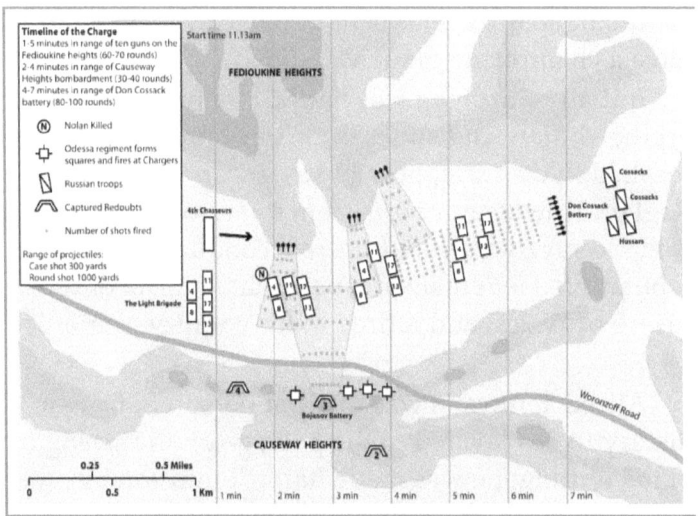

Timeline of the Charge of the Light Brigade showing the "Valley of Death"

Although it was obvious that "someone had blundered," no protest was raised, and the charge began with Lord Cardigan in the lead. The Light Brigade rode into heavy fire and even reached the Russian guns, but without backup from Lucan's heavy cavalry, they were rapidly repulsed, and retreated with 118 men killed, 127 wounded, and about 60 taken prisoner. Only 195 of the original Light Brigade returned with their horses, including Cardigan.

Lucan's heavy cavalry didn't charge at all, leaving his brother-in-law's force completely exposed. Although Lord Cardigan led the charge, some argue that he actually fled the scene before the Light Brigade hit the Russian line. After the battle, Cardigan boarded his yacht in Balaclava harbor to have a champagne dinner.

Initially Cardigan was hailed as a hero, and his brother-in-law and superior officer Lucan was recalled in disgrace, possibly as a scapegoat for Raglan. However, reports from numerous Light Brigade survivors about his real conduct eroded his reputation. He remained a personal favorite of the Prince of Wales, and retired to his country estate.

Alfred Tennyson was the first person in British history to be elevated to the peerage on the strength of his writing; he was made Baron Tennyson by Queen Victoria. He is the ninth most frequently quoted writer in *The Oxford Dictionary of Quotations*.

Thomas Edison made a recording of Tennyson reciting his own poem on a wax cylinder in 1890; it can be found on the Wikipedia page devoted to the poem or on YouTube at http://www.youtube.com/watch?v=MkqUq26z1CE.

December 9 Holidays and Celebrations

Aninden (Bulgaria)

In some folk legends and New Testament apocrypha, St. Anna is the mother of the Virgin Mary, and thus the protector of marriage, virginity, pregnant women, and widows. It is also the name day for women named Anna (or variations thereof).

In Bulgarian custom, women rub the udders of cows, sheep, and goats with wood ashes, garlic, and fat. A plate of salt and wheat, covered with a white cloth, is kept under the oven overnight and fed to the cattle the next day. Women are not supposed to work and men are supposed to stay in their villages so that mermaids don't fall in love with them. In the evening, men burn dry ox dung in front of the front door to keep away evil spirits.

Anna's Day (Sweden and Finland)

St. Anna's Day in Sweden and Finland marks the day that people begin to prepare lutefisk to be consumed on Christmas Eve. As with the Bulgarian Aninden festival, it is also the name day for all people named Anna.

Christmas Card Day

December 9 is Christmas Card Day, in honor of Sir Henry Cole (1818-1874), an Englishman who created the first commercial Christmas card in 1843.

The first commercial Christmas card

Independence Day (Tanzania)

Tanzanian Independence Day commemorates the independence of Tanganyika from Great Britain in 1961.

International Anti-Corruption Day (United Nations)

The UN Convention Against Corruption designated December 9 as International Anti-Corruption Day, focusing on how corruption undermines democracy and the rule of law and erodes the quality of life.

National Heroes Day (Antigua and Barbuda)

Formerly known as V. C. Bird Day, celebrating the first prime minister of the country, who was declared a national hero, National Heroes Day in Antigua and Barbuda celeberates the lives of the country's heroes who by example and contribution changed the history of the nation for the better.

National Pastry Day (United States)

In the United States, almost every day of the year is dedicated to a particular food. Sponsored by manufacturers, retailers, farmers, or simply fans, these days are often proclaimed by the President, Congress, state governors, or mayors.

December 9 is National Pastry Day. The term "pastry" applies to various baked products, ranging from small tarts to pies and quiches. Pastry has a higher fat content than bread, which gives it its flaky or crumbly texture. Pastry dates back to antiquity; Romans, Greeks, Phoenicians, and Egyptians all produced pastries. In the Orient, pastries made with rice rather than wheat are common.

Юрьев день (Yuriev Den) (Russian Orthodox Church)

St. George, known in Russian as St. Yuri, has two feast day. *Vesenniy Yuriev Den* (Yuri's Day in the Spring) is celebrated on April 23 in the Julian calendar, which translates as May 6 in the Gregorian calendar, which is the date of St. George's Day in other Christian denominations. (See On Dates, page 80, for an explanation of Julian and Gregorian calendars.)

In Russia, *Osenniy Yuriev Den* (Yuri's Day in the Autumn) commemorates the consecration of the Church of St. George in Kiev on November 26 (Julian), 1051, which is December 9 in the Gregorian system. Because Yuri's Day in the Autumn occurs when the agricultural year is over and the harvest was in, Russian serfs were allowed a two-week window to move from one landowner to another.

This privilege was stopped around 1600 by Boris Godunov, leading to the Russian expression, "There you have it, Yuri's referring to broken promises or failed expectations.

Christian Feast Days

In **Western Christianity**, December 9 is the feast day of Juan Diego, Loecadia, Nectarius of Auvergne, and Peter Fourier.

In **Eastern Orthodox Christianity**, December 9 is the Feast of the Conception of the Most Holy Theotokos by St. Anna, the Prophetess Hannah (mother of the Prophet Samuel), Saint Vassa, Saint Sophronius, and Saint Stephen of Constantinople. (These events are observed on December 22 by "Old Calendarists.")

What Happened on December 9?

1531 — Virgin of Guadalupe Appears

According to Catholic tradition, a young Native American named Juan Diego witnessed an apparition of the Virgin Mary appear on four separate occasions, beginning December 9, 1531, marked by an image of the Virgin appearing on his cloak. Juan Diego was made a saint, and a shrine to this miracle, the Basilica of Our Lady of Guadalupe in México City, is one of the most visited shrines in the world, and the Virgin of Guadalupe (*Nuestra Señora de Guadalupe*) is considered the symbol of Catholic Mexicans.

1824 — Battle of Ayacucho

The Battle of Ayacucho (also known as the Battle of La Quinua) was the decisive battle of the Peruvian War of Independence and was a key moment in the independence movement for all of South America. Fought between a Spanish Royalist army under the command of the Viceroy La Serna and José de Canterac and an Independentist army consisting of Peruvian, Colombian, Chilean, and other forces, the final capitulation of the Royalist forces all but eliminated Spain's ability to dominate its South American possessions.

Saint Juan Diego witnessing the Virgin of Guadalupe,
by Miguel Cabrero

1872 — First US African-American Governor

On December 9, 1872, P. B. S. Pinchback became the 24th Governor of the state of Louisiana, the first person of African-American descent to become governor of a US state. Pinchback was a member of the Louisiana Senate who became acting lieutenant governor on the death of Oscar Dunn, the first elected African-American lieutenant governor of a US state. The Louisiana legislature had filed impeachment charges against the incumbent governor, who was required under state law to step aside until the outcome was reached. Pinchback was governor for 35 days until the end of the governor's term. Later, Pinchback became the first African-American elected to the US House of Representatives from Louisiana.

P. B. S. Pinchback (Photo: Mathew Brady or Levin Corbin Handy)

1946 — The Doctors' Trial

Following the war crimes trials of leading Nazi officials at Nuremberg, a second set of trials began December 9, 1946, known variously as the "Doctors' Trial" or the "Subsequent Nuremberg Trials." Of the 23 defendants, 20 were medical doctors accused of human experimentation and mass murder. (The most infamous, Josef Mengele, had evaded capture and was therefore not among the defendants.) Seven of the defendants were acquitted, seven were sentenced to death, and the remainder received sentences ranging from ten years to life.

A death sentence is pronounced on Karl Brandt, Hitler's personal physician and Reich Commissar for Health and Sanitation, at the Doctors' Trial. He was hanged in 1948.

1946 — First Session of the Constitutent Assembly of India

As the move toward independence of India from Great Britain gathered steam, a Constituent Assembly of indirectly elected representatives was established to draft a constitution for India (which at the time still included what became Pakistan and Bangladesh).

Meeting for the first time on December 9, 1946, the Constituent Assembly worked until June 1947, when the delegations from Sindh, East Bengal, Baluchistan, West Punjab, and the North West Frontier Province withdrew to form the Constituent Assembly of Pakistan.

The Constituent Assembly of India finally produced a constitution that went into effect on January 26, 1950, a day now celebrated in India as Republic Day.

1960 —The Longest Running Soap Opera Begins Broadcasting

Coronation Street, a British television soap opera, began broadcasting on December 9, 1960. As of Sepember 17, 2010, it became the world's longest-running TV soap opera in production.

1961 —Tanganyika Gains Independence

On December 9, 1961, the Republic of Tanganyika became independent from Great Britain, first as a Commonwealth realm, and exactly one year later a republic within the Commonwealth of Nations.

In 1964, Tanganyika and Zanzibar formed the United Republic of Tanganyika and Zanzibar, which changed its name the following year to the United Republic of Tanzania. As a colony, the Tanganyika Territory had been part of German East Africa, taken by the British under a League of Nations Mandate in 1922. The other parts of German East Africa were taken by Belgium, and are today known as the nations of Rwanda and Burundi.

1962 —The Petrified Forest National Park is Established

On December 9, 1962, the Petrified Forest in northeastern Arizona, noted for its large deposits of petrified wood, was upgraded from the status of national monument, which it had received in 1906, to become a national park under the jurisdiction of the National Park Service. Over half a million people visit the park, which covers nearly 150 square miles, each year.

1965 —Kecksburg UFO Incident

On the night of December 9, 1965, thousands of people in six US states and Ontario, Canada, witnessed a large fireball that streaked over Detroit, dropped hot metal over Michigan on northern Ohio, caused some grass fires and sonic booms in western Pennsylvania, and finally crashed in Kecksburg, Pennsylvania, about 30 miles southeast of Pittsburgh. The US Army, Project Blue Book, state police, and NASA investigated, and classified the event as a mid-sized meteor.

Petrified Forest National Park

(Kecksburg, continued) In 2005, NASA reclassified the event as a re-entering Soviet satellite. However, varying theories point out discrepancies and strange events in the official record, and many belive it was an alien spacecraft or possibly a secret Nazi experiment. The Kecksburg UFO Incident is sometimes referred to as Pennsylvania's Roswell, referencing the famous 1948 UFO sighting near Roswell, New Mexico.

1965 —*A Charlie Brown Christmas* Debuts

The perennial Christmas television special, *A Charlie Brown Christmas*, premiered on CBS television on December 9, 1965, and has aired during the Christmas season every year since.

Image from *A Charlie Brown Christmas* (© and ™)

1979 —Smallpox Eradicated

On December 9, 1979, a commission of scientists reporting to the United Nations World Health Organization (WHO) reported that smallpox, which was killing as many as 2 million people a year as recently as 1959, had been eradicated in nature.

The last naturally occuring case of indigenous smallpox occurred in 1977; a medical photographer in 1978 contracted smallpox in a research institution. Subsequently, all remaining smallpox stocks were transferred to two highly secure research laboratories.

1987 —First Intifada Begins

On December 9, 1987, increasing tension between Palestinians and Israelis boiled over at the Jabalia refugee camp, triggering what became known as the First Intifada, a Palestinian uprising against Israeli occupation. The violence and civil disobedience lasted six years.

Deaths included 1,087 Palestinians killed by Israeli security forces and 160 Israelis (military and civilian) killed by Palestinians. Following the Oslo Accords, the violence subsided, but broke out again in the Second Intifada, which began in September 2000 and lasted another five years.

2008 —Illinois Governor Rod Blagojevich Arrested

Rod Blagojevich, 40th governor of Illinois, was arrested on December 9, 2008 (the day before his birthday), for various crimes including the solicitation of bribes for political appointments, including the vacant US Senate seat previously occupied by Barack Obama upon his election to the US Presidency. Blagojevich was convicted and in March 2012 began serving a 14-year prison term.

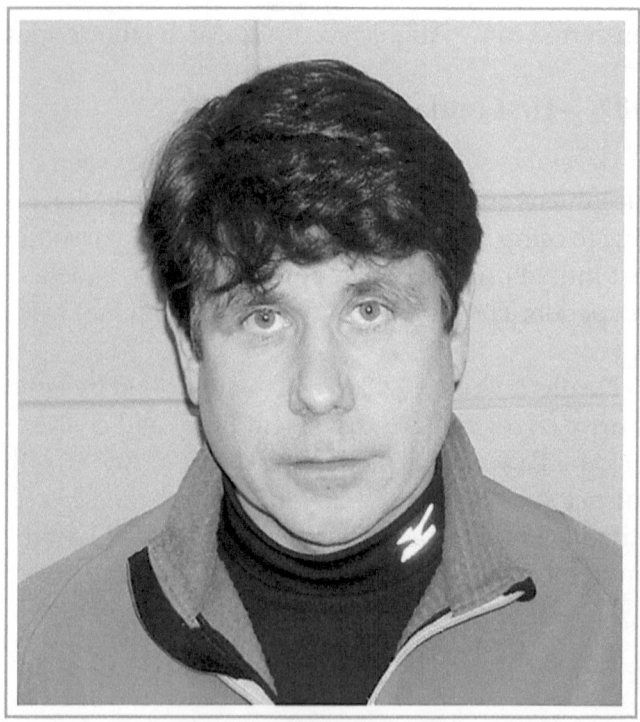

Mug shot of Rod Blagojevich

Who Was Born on December 9?

Adventure

Max Manus (December 9, 1914 — September 20, 1996)

Norwegian World War II resistance fighter Max Manus was considered one of the most brilliant saboteurs during the war. He wrote several books about his adventures, including *Det Vil Helst Gå Godt (It Usually Ends Well)*. He was the subject of the 2008 Norwegian film *Max Manus: Man of War*. Following the war, he built a successful office supply business.

Jean Mermoz (December 9, 1901 — December 7, 1936)

French aviator Jean Mermoz gained his initial reputation with the French Air Force in Syria in the 1920s. He became an airmail pilot flying dangerous routes through North Africa (he was captured by Tuareg rebels after one crash, but was rescued). He was the main pilot on a new direct airline between France and South America, and helped create Aerolíneas Argentinas.

Along with his associate Antoine de Saint-Exupéry (himself famous for his book *The Little Prince*), he is considered one of the most important men in the history of Argentine commercial aviation. He was lost at sea when an engine on his Laté 300 airplane failed. A film, *Mermoz*, chronicles his career.

Business

Clarence Birdseye (December 9, 1886 — October 7, 1956)

Taxidermist and entrepreneur Clarence Birdseye began researching improved methods of fast-freezing food, leading to the company that bears his name: Birds Eye Frozen Food. He is considered the founder of the modern frozen food industry.

Government and Military

Crown Princess Masako (皇太子徳仁親王妃雅子) (December 9, 1947 —)

Crown Princess Masako of Japan is the wife of Crown Prince Naruhito, heir apparent to the Chyrsanthemum Throne.

Tom Daschle (December 9, 1947 —)

Tom Daschle was US Senator from South Dakota from 1987 to 2005, and Senate Majority Leader from 2001 to 2003.

Sonia Gandhi (December 9, 1946 —)

Italian-born Indian politician Sonia Gandhi was married to assassinated Indian prime minister Rajiv Gandhi. Following his death, she became President of the Indian National Congress Party in 1998.

James Jesus Angleton (December 9, 1917 — May 12, 1987)

James Jesus Angleton was one of the founding senior officers of the US Central Intelligence Agency. A highly influential figure in US intelligence, he ran the CIA counterintelligence operation from 1954 to 1975, serving under six CIA directors.

Tip O'Neill (December 9, 1912 — January 5, 1994)

Massachusetts congressman Thomas (Tip) O'Neill (next page) was Speaker of the US House of Representatives for ten years. He was the only Speaker who served for five complete consecutive Congresses, and the second-longest serving Speaker in US history, after Sam Rayburn.

Peter Kropotkin (December 9, 1842 — February 8, 1921)

Born a prince, Pyotr Alexeyevich Kropotkin (Пётр Алексе́евич Кропо́ткин) embraced anarchy and communism, and became an early leader in the Communist movement, traveling through Europe on behalf of the cause. He spent time in jail for advocating anarchy.

Tip O'Neill

(Kropotkin continued) After the February Revolution of 1917 that left Russia with a democratically-elected government, he returned to Russia a hero, only to be disillusioned when the authoritarian Bolsheviks seized power that October. The occasion of his funeral was the last time in Soviet history that anti-Bolshevik anarchists were allowed to demonstrate in public.

Gustavus Adolphus of Sweden (December 9, 1594 — November 6, 1632)

Swedish monarch Gustav II Adolf (normally known by the Latinized version of his name) turned his nation into an empire: *Svenska Stormaktstiden*, a great European power dominating the Balkan region from. At its height, the Swedish Empire dominated Scandinavia, the Balkans and parts of northern Germany, making it the third largest nation in Europe.

Gustavus Adolphus became king in 1611, when he was only seventeen years old. He showed an innate talent for military leadership, and made innovations in tactical integration of infantry, cavalry, logistics, and artillery. Napoléon Bonaparte, George S. Patton, and Carl von Clausewitz all named him as one of the greatest generals of all time, and he is often referred to as the "Father of Modern Warfare."

During the Thirty Years War, he defeated a Catholic army in the Battle of Breitenfeld, giving the Protestants their first major military victory and stopping the Catholic attempt to reconvert the German nations.

Known in his day as "The Golden King" and "The Lion of the North," Gustavus Adolphus was killed at the Battle of Lützen at the age of 38. After his death, the Swedish Riksdag added "the Great" to his name, the only Swedish ruler so honored. The day of his death, November 6, is celebrated as Gustavus Adolphus Day in Sweden.

Gustavus Adolphus at the Battle of Breitenfeld, Johann Walter (1632)

Music

Jakob Dylan (December 9, 1969 —)

Singer-songwriter Jakob Dylan is the son of musician Bob Dylan. He is the lead singer of The Wallflowers, and has recorded two solo albums.

Donny Osmond (December 9, 1957 —)

Former teen idol Donny Osmond began as the youngest member of The Osmonds, had numerous hits including "Go Away Little Girl" and "Puppy Love," and co-starred with his sister Marie in the variety television series Donny & Marie.

Joan Armatrading (December 9, 1950 —)

British singer-songwriter Joan Armatrading has had six gold records out of 18 studio albums.

Dennis Dunaway (December 9, 1946 —)

Musician Dennis Dunaway is known as a member of the band Alice Cooper and wrote their hit song "School's Out."

Neil Innes (December 9, 1944 —)

Comic song creator and performer Neil Innes is known for his work with the Monty Python troupe and as a member of the Bonzo Dog Doo-Dah Band and The Rutles.

Dan Hicks (December 9, 1941 —)

Singer-songwriter Dan Hicks is known for such tunes as "I Scare Myself," "Canned Music," and "How Can I Miss You When You Won't Go Away?" He was the leader of the band Dan Hicks & His Hot Licks.

David Houston (December 9, 1935 — November 30, 1993)

Country music singer-songwriter David Houston had numerous number-one singles in the 1960s and 1970s, and received two Grammy Awards.

Performing Arts

Reiko Aylesworth (December 9, 1972 —)

Reiko Aylesworth is best known for her role as Michelle Dessler on the television series 24.

Felicity Huffman (December 9, 1962 —)

Felicity Huffman earned a Golden Globe nomination for her role in the television series *Sports Night*, and won an Emmy for playing Lynette Scavo on *Desperate Housewives*. She received an Academy Award nomination for Best Actress for her role in the independent film *Transamerica*.

Joe Lando (December 9, 1961 —)

Joe Lando is best known for playing Jake Harrison in *One Life to Live* and Byron Sully in *Dr. Quinn, Medicine Woman.*

John Malkovich (December 9, 1953 —)

John Malkovich received Academy Award nominations for his roles in *Places in the Heart* and *In the Line of Fire*, and appeared in starring roles in such films as *Dangerous Liaisons*, *Of Mice and Men*, and *Being John Malkovich* as a fictionalized version of himself.

Michael Dorn (December 9, 1952 —)

Michael Dorn is best known for his role as Worf, a Klingon in the *Star Trek* franchise.

Michael Nouri (December 9, 1945 —)

Actor Michael Nouri is best known for his role in the 1983 film *Flashdance.*

Beau Bridges (December 9, 1941 —)

American actor Beau Bridges won three Emmy Awards, two Golden Globes, and a Grammy, appearing in such films as *Norma Rae* (1979), *The Fabulous Baker Boys* (1989), and *The Positively True Adventures of the Alleged Texas Cheerleader-Murdering Mom* (1993). He is the son of actor Lloyd Bridges and the brother of actor Jeff Bridges.

Judi Dench (December 9, 1934 —)

British actress Dame Judi Dench played Queen Victoria
in *Mrs. Brown* (1997), won an Academy Award for Best
Actress for *Shakespeare in Love* (1998), and has had an
acclaimed careeer in theatre. She may be best known
for playing "M" in the James Bond films from 1995 to
2012.

Judi Dench (Photo: Caroline Bonarde Ucci)

Morton Downey Jr. (December 9, 1932 — March 12, 2001)

Morton Downey, Jr., is best known as the host of the eponymous 1980s talk show *The Morton Downey, Jr., Show.*

Buck Henry (December 9, 1930 —)

Buck Henry (Henry Zuckerman) is an actor, writer, and director who is best known for hosting *Saturday Night Live* ten times. He co-created and wrote for the 1960s sitcom *Get Smart* and developed the 1967 series *Captain Nice* and the 1978 series *Quark.*

John Cassavetes (December 9, 1929 — February 3, 1989)

Greek-American actor, director, and writer John Cassavetes (Ιωάννης Κασσαβέτης) is known for his roles in such films as *Rosemary's Baby* (1968) and *The Dirty Dozen* (1967), and wrote and directed over a dozen independent films.

Dick Van Patten (December 9, 1928 —)

Dick Van Patten is best known for his starring role in the 1970s sitcom *Eight Is Enough*. He also founded the company Natural Balance Pet Foods.

Dina Merrill (December 9, 1923 —)

Only child of heiress Marjorie Merriweather Post, actress Dina Merrill received a lifetime achievement award from the American Academy of Dramatic Arts for her roles in such films as *Desk Set* (1957), *Operation Petticoat* (1959), *Butterfield 8* (1960), and *The Courtship of Eddie's Father* (1963). In addition, she had a business career as an executive of RKO Pictures and served on the board of the John F. Kennedy Center for the Performing Arts.

Redd Foxx (December 9, 1922 — October 11, 1991)

Under his stage name Redd Foxx, American comedian John Sanford gained initial fame for his explicit nightclub act and a series of comedy albums, and starred in the 1970s sitcom *Sanford and Son*. He is ranked among the greatest stand-up comics of all time by Comedy Central.

Kirk Douglas (December 9, 1916 —)

Actor Kirk Douglas (left, with Lauren Bacall), born Issur Danielovitch (Иссур Даниелович), is ranked #17 on the American Film Institute's list of the greatest male screen legends in American film history.

His notable films include *Young Man With a Horn* (1950), *Lust for Life* (1956), *Gunfight at the O.K. Corral* (1957), and *Spartacus* (1960). He is the father of actor Michael Douglas.

Frances Reid (December 9, 1914 — February 3, 2010)

Frances Reid is best remembered for her long-running role as Alice Horton on the soap opera *Days of Our Lives* from 1965 to 2007.

Broderick Crawford (December 9, 1911 — April 26, 1986)

Broderick Crawford won the Academy Award for Best Actor for his role as Governor Willie Stark in the 1949 film *All the King's Men*, and starred in the 1950s television series *Highway Patrol*.

Douglas Fairbanks, Jr. (December 9, 1909 — May 7, 2000)

Son of swashbuckling star Douglas Fairbanks, Fairbanks Jr. became a noted actor in his own right in such films as 1930's *The Dawn Patrol*, 1937's *Prisoner of Zenda*, and 1939's *Gunga Din*.

During World War II, he had a distinguished military career, receiving a Silver Star for valor along with many other medals.

He also has three stars on the Hollywood Walk of Fame and is a member of the Hall of Fame of the International Best Dressed List.

Margaret Hamilton (December 9, 1902 — May 16, 1985)

American character actress Margaret Hamilton (next page) is best known for her role as the Wicked Witch of the West in the 1939 film *The Wizard of Oz*.

Margaret Hamilton (left) with Judy Garland in *The Wizard of Oz*

Emmett Kelly (December 9, 1898 — March 28, 1979)

Ringling Brothers and Barnum & Bailey Circus clown Emmett Kelly was famous for his hobo character "Weary Willie," who would try to sweep up the spotlight circle at the end of a circus act. He played his character in Cecil B. DeMille's 1952 film *The Greatest Show on Earth.*

Emmett Kelly (Photo: Joseph Steinmetz)

Hermione Gingold (December 9, 1897 — May 24, 1987)

Hermione Gingold is best known for her roles as a strong-willed elderly character in such films as *Gigi; Bell, Book and Candle;* and *The Music Man.*

Tim Moore (December 9, 1887 — December 13, 1958)

African-American vaudeville comedian Tim Moore is best known for his role as George "Kingfish" Stevens in the television sitcom *Amos 'n' Andy.*

From left to right, Alvin Childress (Amos), **Tim Moore** (Kingfish), and Spencer Williams (Andy) from Amos 'n' Andy (1952)

Science and Technology

Henry Way Kendall (December 9, 1926 — February 15, 1999)

American particle physicist Henry Kendall shared the 1990 Nobel Prize in Physics for pioneering work in support of the quark model of particle physics.

William Lipscomb (December 9, 1919 — April 24, 2011)

American chemist William Lipscomb won the 1976 Nobel Prize in Chemistry for his work on the molecular structure of borane compounds.

James Rainwater (December 9, 1917 — May 31, 1986)

American physicist James Rainwater shared the 1975 Nobel Prize in Physics for his work in determining the asymmetrical shapes of certain atomic nuclei.

Grace Hopper (December 9, 1906 — January 1, 1992)

US Navy Admiral and pioneering computer scientist Grace Hopper is credited as the conceptualizer of what became COBOL, one of the first modern programming languages. She worked on a number of pioneering projects in the early days of mechanical computing, and has been recognized in numerous ways for her achievements.

She is credited with coining the phrase "debugging," based on actually removing a moth stuck in a relay, and with the famous adage, "It's easier to ask forgiveness than it is to get permission."

Grace Hopper (center) in front of the UNIVAC computer, circa 1960

Fritz Haber (December 9, 1868 — January 29, 1934)

German chemist Fritz Haber won the 1918 Nobel Prize in Chemistry for developing a method of synthesizing ammonia, and is known as the "father of chemical warfare."

Sports

McKayla Maroney (December 9, 1995 —)

Gymnast McKayla Maroney won an individual silver medal and shared a team gold medal at the 2012 London Olympics. A photograph of her with a slightly disappointed look with her lips pursed to the side became an Internet viral phenomenon called "McKayla is not impressed."

McKayla Maroney with her "not impressed" expression
(White HousePhoto: Pete Souza)

Kurt Angle (December 9, 1968 —)

Kurt Angle won an Olympic gold medal in wrestling and was named one of the top 15 college wrestlers of all time by USA Wrestling. He is the only Olympic gold medalist to become a professional wrestler, working with Total Nonstop Action Wrestling and World Wrestling Federation/Entertainment, where he earned numerous championship titles.

World B. Free (December 9, 1953 —)

Basketball player Lloyd B. Free played in the NBA from 1975 to 1988. He changed his name legally to "World" in 1981.

Tom Kite (December 9, 1949 —)

Golfer and golf course designer Tom Kite was named to the World Golf Hall of Fame in 2004.

Dick Butkus (December 9, 1942 —)

Chicago Bears linebacker Dick Butkus was named to the Pro Football Hall of Fame in 1979.

Billy Bremner (December 9, 1942 — December 7, 1997)

Scottish professional footballer (soccer player) Billy Bremner captained the Leeds United team in the 1960s and 1970. He is a member of the English Football Hall of Fame and the Scottish Football Hall of Fame.

Deacon Jones (December 9, 1938 — June 3, 2013)

Football defensive end Deacon Jones played for the Los Angeles Rams, the San Diego Chargers, and the Washington Redskins, and was inducted into the Pro Football Hall of Fame in 1980. He coined the term "sack."

Hannes Kolehmainen (December 9, 1889 — January 11, 1966)

Finnish long-distance runner Hannes Kolehmainen won three gold medals in the 1912 Stockholm Olympics and another gold in the 1920 Antwerp games. He moved to the United States, where he continued to compete, and became a US citizen in 1921.

Joseph Pilates (December 9, 1883 — October 9, 1967)

German-American gymnast Joseph Pilates overcame poor childhood health through physical fitness. He developed the exercise method known as Pilates.

Harry Miller (December 9, 1875 — May 3, 1943)

From 1923 to 1928, race car designer and builder Harry Miller built nine cars that won the Indianapolis 500, and engines for three other cars that won the race — an astounding 83 percent of Indy 500 winners!

Joe Kelley (December 9, 1871 — August 14, 1943)

Known as the "Kingpin of the Orioles," left-fielder Joe Kelley was named to the National Baseball Hall of Fame in 1971.

Baltimore Orioles players, circa 1895. Standing (l-r): Wee Willie Keeler and John T. McGraw. Seated (l-r): **Joe Kelley** and Hugh Jennings

Words

Ashleigh Brilliant (December 9, 1933 —)

Humorist and cartoonist Ashleigh Brilliant is known for his one-line epigrams, such as "I may not be totally perfect, but parts of me are excellent" and "I have abandoned my search for truth and am now looking for a good fantasy."

Humayun Mirza (December 9, 1928 —)

Humayun Mirza is the son of Iskander Mirza, first President of Pakistan, and the last of the royal line of Mughal rulers of Bengal, Bihar, and Orissa. He wrote *From Plassey to Pakistan* (published by Timespinner Press), a history of the Indian subcontinent through the British Raj, Partition, and the founding of Pakistan, as seen through the eyes of his royal ancestors. Following a coup against his father in 1958, Mirza spent his career as an executive of the World Bank, with major responsibilities through Central and South America as well as Nigeria.

Humayun Mirza (Photo: Michael Dobson)

Eloise Jarvis McGraw (December 9, 1915 — November 30, 2000)

Children's book author Eloise Jarvis McGraw received three Newbery Honor awards and an Edgar Award for Best Juvenile Mystery. She is also known for her Oz books continuing the series started by L. Frank Baum.

Dalton Trumbo (December 9, 1905 — September 10, 1976)

Screenwriter and novelist Dalton Trumbo (right, with Bertolt Brecht in the background) was one of the Hollywood Ten, cited for contempt of Congress and blacklisted for refusing to answer questions from the House Un-American Actitivies Committee (HUAC) about alleged Communist involvement.

He continued to work under pseudonyms, and won two Academy Awards as screenwriter for *Exodus* and *Spartacus*. As a novelist, he is known for his 1939 novel *Johnny Got His Gun*, which won a National Book Award.

Jean de Brunhoff (December 9, 1899 — October 16, 1937)

French writer and illustrator Jean de Brunhoff is best known for his series of children's books featuring Babar the Elephant.

Illustration from *The Story of Babar* (1931), by Jean de Brunhoff

Joel Chandler Harris (December 9, 1848 — July 3, 1908)

Journalist and folklorist Joel Chandler Harris was best known for interpreting African-American oral storytelling traditions into the "Brer Rabbit" stories, attributed to "Uncle Remus."

Known as Joe Harris in normal life, he was an editor at the *Atlanta Constitution* newspaper, and actively promoted racial reconciliation and African-American equality in that role.

The Disney movie *Song of the South* is based on his Uncle Remus stories.

John Milton (December 9, 1608 — November 8, 1674)

English poet John Milton is best known for his epic work *Paradise Lost*, which retells the Biblical story of the expulsion of Adam and Even from the Garden of Eden.

Allied with the Puritans during the English Civil War, he became a civil servant in the Cromwell-led Commonwealth government, serving as "Secretary of Foreign Tongues." He wrote numerous polemics in defense of the Commonwealth and disparaging the monarchy. When the monarchy was restored in 1660, Milton was briefly arrested, but eventually pardoned.

He went blind by 1654. Living in poverty, he dictated *Paradise Lost* to his daughters and others who would transcribe it. The work was first published in 1664 and is now considered one of the great classic works in the English language.

Two other important Milton works, *Paradise Regained* and *Samson Agonistes*, followed.
Milton died at the age of 62.

A blind John Milton dictates Paradise Lost to his daughters, by Eugène Delacroix (c. 1826)

Self portrait by Anthony van Dyck

Who Died on December 9?

Art and Illustration

Anthony van Dyck (March 22, 1599 — December 9, 1641)

Flemish baroque artist Anthony van Dyke is famous for his portraits of Charles I of England. The Van dyke (or Vandyke), a type of short, pointed beard, is named for him, as is the Cavalier period dress costume seen on Gainsborough's famous *Blue Boy* portrait.

Aviation

Douglas "Wrong Way" Corrigan (January 2, 1907 — December 9, 1996)

Aviator Douglas Corrigan is best known for his unauthorized 1938 flight from New York to Ireland, after filing a flight plan to fly to Long Beach, California. He claimed that a navigational error resulting from a heavy cloud cover led him to misread his compass.

Although there was great skepticism of his claim, he never publicly admitted to flying across the Atlantic deliberately, and earned the nickname "Wrong Way" for his feat.

A skilled aircraft mechanic, Corrigan earlier in his career helped build Charles Lindbergh's *Spirit of St. Louis* for the Ryan Aeronautical Company.

Douglas "Wrong Way" Corrigan

Artem Mikoyan (August 5, 1905 [O.S. July 23] — December 9, 1970)

Aircraft designer Artem Mikoyan (Артём Микоян) co-founded the Mikoyan-Gurevich Design Bureau, responsible for the MiG series of Soviet military aircraft, from the MiG-1 through MiG-25. [For an explanation of "O. S.," see page 80.]

Government and Politics

Paul Simon (November 29, 1928 — December 9, 2003)

Illinois politician Paul Simon served ten years in the US House of Representatives and twelve years in the US Senate and ran unsuccessfully for the 1988 Democratic presidential nomination.

Leon Jaworski (September 19, 1905 — December 9, 1982)

Leon Jaworski was appointed the second special prosecutor during the Watergate Scandal, replacing Archibald Cox who was dismissed in the "Saturday Night Massacre."

Ralph Bunche (August 7, 1903 or 1904 — December 9, 1971)

American diplomat and academic Ralph Bunche (next page) was the first person of color to receive the Nobel Peace Prize, winning it in 1950 for his mediation in Palestine. He was involved in the formation of the United Nations, was an activist in the American civil rights movement, and became Undersecretary-General of the UN in 1968, serving until health problems forced him to resign.

Ralph Bunche

Feroz Khan Noon (May 7, 1893 — December 9, 1970)

Malik Sir Feroz Khan Noon was the seventh Prime Minister of Pakistan, serving under the presidency of Iskander Mirza. He had previously been one of pre-Partition India's delegates to the San Francisco conference that established the United Nations and was the special envoy of Pakistan founder Muhammad Ali Jinnah when Pakistan became independent.

Enoch L. Johnson (January 20, 1883 — December 9, 1968)

Enoch "Nucky" Johnson ran the political machine that ruled Atlantic City, New Jersey, during the Roaring Twenties, and was involved with bootlegging, gambling, and prostitution. He was convicted of racketeering in 1941 and served four years in prison. In the HBO television series *Boardwalk Empire*, Steve Buscemi played a fictionalized version of Johnson named "Nucky Thompson."

Music

Jenni Rivera (July 2, 1969 — December 9, 2012)

Jenni Rivera was known for her *banda* and *norteña* recordings, with numerous #1 hits on the Latin charts.

Patty Donahue (March 29, 1956 — December 9, 1996)

Patty Donahue was the lead singer of the 1980s new wave group The Waitresses.

Performing Arts

Gene Barry (June 14, 1919 — December 9, 2009)

Actor Gene Barry was best known for his roles as the title characters in the TV series *Bat Masterson* and *Burke's Law.*

Gene Barry (Photo: Elmer Holloway)

Vincent Gardenia (January 7, 1920 — December 9, 1992)

Actor Victor Gardenia received Academy Award nominations for Best Supporting Actor for his roles in *Bang the Drum Slowly* (1973) and *Moonstruck* (1987). He was also known for playing Archie Bunker's neighbor Frank on the sitcom *All in the Family,* and for his role as J. Edgar Hoover in the 1983 miniseries *Kennedy.*

William A. Wellman (February 29, 1896 — December 9, 1975)

Director William A. Wellman worked on over 80 films throughout his long career. He is best known for his 1927 film *Wings,* which won the first Academy Award for Best Picture.

Poster for Wings

Religion

Fulton J. Sheen (May 8, 1895 — December 9, 1979)

American Catholic Archbishop Fulton J. Sheen is
known as one of the first televangelists for his radio
and television ministry beginning with the 1930-1950
radio program *The Catholic Hour* and the television
programs *Life Is Worth Living* (1951-1957) and *The
Fulton Sheen Program* (1961-1968). A case for his
sainthood was begun in 2002.

Fulton J. Sheen

Science and Technology

N. Joseph Woodland (September 6, 1921 — December 9, 2012)

Engineer Joseph Woodland co-invented the barcode, which received US Patent 2,612,994 in 1952.

Patrick Moore (March 4, 1923 — December 9, 2012)

British amateur astronomer Patrick Moore was best known as presenter of the BBC television series *The Sky at Night* from 1957 to 2013, the longest-running television program with the same presenter in history.

Mary Leakey (February 6, 1913 — December 9, 1996)

Paleoanthropologist Mary Leakey discovered important early hominid fossils including the first *Proconsul* skull and a *Zinjanthropous* skull in the Olduvai Gorge, as well as fifteen new species and one new genus of animals. She was married to and a partner with anthropologist Louis Leakey.

Gustaf Dalén (March 22, 1869 — December 9, 1937)

Swedish industrialist Gustaf Dalén received the 1912 Nobel Prize in Physics for the innovative sun valve that allowed automatic operation of carbide gas-powered lights used in lighthouses, known as Dalén lights.

Sports

Archie Moore (December 13, 1916 — December 9, 1998)

Boxer Archie "The Old Mongoose" Moore was World Light Heavyweight Champion from 1952 to 1962 and had one of the longest professional careers in boxing history. He is ranked #4 on The Ring's list of "100 Greatest Punchers of All Time." He was also an active civil rights figure and a character actor in television and film.

Branch Rickey (December 20, 1881 — December 9, 1965)

After a brief career as a catcher, Branch Rickey served as a manager and executive for the St. Louis Browns, St. Louis Cardinals, New York Yankees, Brooklyn Dodgers, and Pittsburgh Pirates. He broke the MLB color barrier by signing African-American player Jackie Robinson, and for drafting the first Afro-Hispanic superstar, Roberto Clemente. He created the framework for the modern minor league farm system and introduced the batting helmet. Nicknamed "The Mahatma," he was elected to the Baseball Hall of Fame in 1967.

Rube Foster (September 17, 1879 — December 9, 1930)

Negro League baseball player and manager Rube Foster founded and managed the Chicago American Giants and the Negro National League, earning the title of "father of Black Baseball." He was elected to the Baseball Hall of Fame in 1981.

Words

Robert Sheckley (July 16, 1928 — December 9, 2005)

Award-winning science fiction writer Robert Sheckley was known for his humorous and absurdist short stories. He won numerous awards, and his 1963 short story "Seventh Victim" was turned into the 1965 film *The 10th Victim (La Decima Vittima),* starring Ursula Andress and Marcello Mastroianni.

Louella Parsons (August 6, 1881 — December 9, 1972)

Pioneering movie columnist Louella Parsons was known as the "Queen of Hollywood" for her influential writing; her columns appeared in over 400 newspapers and were read by 20 million people. She was known for her long-running feud with competitor Hedda Hopper.

Edith Sitwell (September 7, 1887 — December 9, 1964)

Poet and critic Dame Edith Sitwell is considered one of the most important voices of twentieth century English poetry. She is best known as the author of the *Façade* poems, set to music by William Walton in a famous 1923 production.

Portrait of Edith Sitwell by Roger Fry (1915)

December: The Twelfth Month

"In cold December fragrant chaplets blow,
And heavy harvests nod beneath the snow."

— Alexander Pope, *Dunciad*.

In Latin, *decem* means "ten," so it may seem strange that December is actually the twelfth month of the year. The original Roman calendar, from which our month names come, began in March, making December indeed the tenth month.

No one is completely sure when the start of the year was moved to January, but the traditional name of December stuck.

In the northern hemisphere, December is the month with the shortest daylight hours of the year; in the southern hemisphere, it's the opposite. December is the equivalent of June in the southern hemisphere, and vice versa.

In the Julian and Gregorian calendars, December is the twelfth and last month of the year, and is one of seven months with 31 days.

In every year, December starts on the same day of the week as September, and ends on the same day of the week as April.

The length of the day varies through the year, because the Earth tilts as it revolves around the Sun. The two extremes are known as the *solstices*, and the points at which day and night are of equal length are known as the *equinoxes*. The northern hemisphere's winter solstice, which is the shortest day of the year, falls in December. In the southern hemisphere, the summer solstice, the longest day of the year, falls in December.

The dates of the solstice can vary between December 20 and 22. Because even the ancients could tell when the days stopped getting shorter (or longer) and started in the other direction, many holidays and festivals take place around the time of the solstice, including most famously Christmas.

December in Other Cultures

In Albanian, the month of December is known as *Dhjetor*. In Egyptian Arabic, it's ديسمبر (pronounced *dīsambar*). In Czech, it's *Prosinec*, in Finland it's *Joulukuu*, and in Poland it's *Grudzień*. Hungarians say *Karácsony hava*.

In Greek, the month of Δεκέμβριος is pronounced *Dekémbrios*. In Hebrew, it's דצמבר and Hindi, it's दिसंबर.

In Irish Gaelic, the month of December is *Nollaig mi na Nollag* and in Scottish Gaelic it's *an Dùbhlachd*. The Welsh say *Rhagfyr*.

The Chinese and Japanese both write the month 十二月, but it is pronounced differently in

Cantonese, Mandarin, and Japanese. Koreans write it as 십이월, or *Sipiweol*. In Vietnam it's 腦迣缸 *(Tháng mươï hai)*.

In Old English, the month is *Gēolmōnaþ* and in Anglo-Saxon it's *Ærra-ǧēola mōnaþ*.

The month of December does not correspond exactly with months in other calendar systems. The Hebrew months of כִּסְלֵו (*Kislev*) and טֵבֵת (*Tevet*) overlap December, as do the Persian months of آذر (*Azar*) and دی (*Dey*) and the Hindu months of मार्गशीर्ष (*Mārgaśirṣa*) and पूस (*Pauṣa*).

In the Islamic world, the lunar calendar consists of 354 or 355 days, meaning that the months slowly migrate through the year, and over time different months correspond to December.

December Superstitions

- "A green December fills the graveyard."
- "When December snows fall fast, marry and true love will last."
- "A December bride will be fond of novelty, entertaining but extravagant."

December Symbols

Birthstone: December birthstones in various traditions include turquoise, lapiz lazuli, zircon, blue topaz, and tanzanite.

Oil painting on lapis lazuli, *Perseus Rescuing Andromeda*, by Giuseppe Cesari.

Birth Flowers: December's flowers are the narcissus and the holly.

Illustration by Anton Hartinger from *Atlas der Alpenflora* (1882)

December Events

Honorary Months

Presidents, Congresses, and nations around the world issue proclamations recognizing particular months to honor certain causes. Other organizations, less formal in nature, do the same thing. These events generally fall in December. (All US unless noted otherwise.)

- Bingo's Birthday Month (the game, not the dog)
- Food Service Safety Month (Worldwide)
- National Critical Infrastructure Protection Month
- National Egg Nog Month
- National Fruit Cake Month
- National Impaired Driving Prevention Month
- National Sign Up for Summer Camp Month
- National Stress-Free Family Holiday Month
- Safe Toys and Gifts Month
- Spiritual Literacy Month
- Write a Business Plan Month

Moveable and Multi-Day Events

Some events take place over a specific week or time period. Start and finish dates may vary from year to year. Some events occur on different days each year (such as "fourth Saturday of a month").

Advent (Christianity)
The four weeks prior to Christmas are known as the Advent season, a time of expectant waiting and preparation for the celebration of the Nativity of Jesus.

Hanukkah (חֲנֻכָּה) (Judaism)
The Jewish celebration of Hanukkah, also known as the Festival of Lights or the Feast of Dedication, takes place for eight days and nights beginning on the 25th day of Kislev, which varies from late November to late December. It commemorates the rededication of the Second Temple in Jerusalem at the time of the Maccabean Revolt.

Each night of Hanukkah is marked by lighting one branch of the Menorah, a candelabrum with nine branches. In addition to prayers, celebrants eat foods fried or baked in olive oil. Children play with a spinning top known as a dreidel and receive Hanukkah gelt.

18th century painting of a Hanukkah celebration, artist unknown.

Karthikai Deepam (கார்த்திகை விளக்கீடு) (Hindu Tamil)

The Hindu Tamil celebration of Karthikai Deepam takes place in mid-November to mid-December when the moon is in conjunction with the Pleiades *(Karthigai)*. It is a religious festival of lamps and also celebrates the bonding between brothers and sisters.

Lager Beer Week (Secular)

The second week in December is dedicated to lager beer.

Michael Dobson

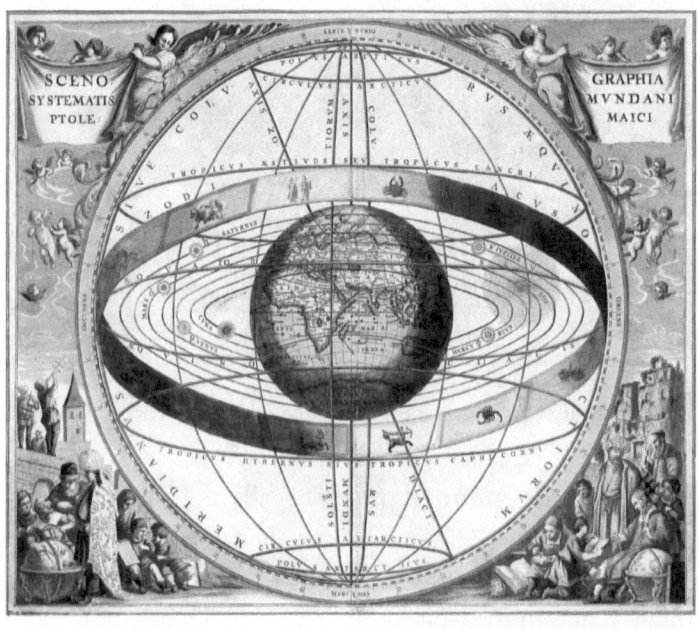

The signs of the zodiac in the Ptolemaic view of the university, by
Johannes van Loon (1660)

December 9 Zodiac Signs

From the perspective of someone on Earth, the Sun appears to move through the sky throughout the year, along a path astronomers call the ecliptic plane. The ecliptic plane is divided into twelve constellations, known as the zodiac, based on traditionally observed patterns of stars. On your birthday, you can't see your constellation, because it's part of the daytime sky.

The zodiac was first developed by Babylonian astronomers about 2,500 years ago. Because they were unaware that the Earth wobbles like a spinning top (a motion known as *precession*), they didn't make allowance for the fact that the Sun's path through the zodiac changes over time.

That means there are now two sets of dates for your birth sign. The *tropical* dates are the original Babylonian dates; the *sidereal* dates tell you where the Sun actually appears as it moves along its annual path.

In tropical reckoning, December 9 is in Sagittarius, and in siderial reckoning, December 9 is in Scorpio.

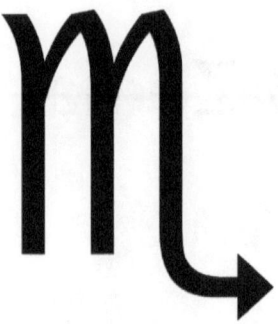

Scorpio

Tropical *October 23 to November 21*

Sidereal *November 16 to December 15*

Scorpio, the Scorpion, appears in the Greek myth of the hunter Orion. Because Orion had touched the robes of the goddess Artemis, in revenge, the goddess had the scorpion kill Orion. As a reward, she placed the scorpion in the sky, where it chases Orion through the eternal night.

The constellation of Scorpius includes the red giant star Antares, which is so large that the entire Solar System through the orbit of Mars would be inside it.

Scorpio is a fire sign, and people born under this sign are supposed to be determined, reserved, loyal, and secretive. Scorpios are supposed to be compatible with the water signs of Pisces and Capricorn.

Sagittarius

Tropical: *November 23 to December 21*
Sidereal: *December 16 to January 14*

Sagittarius means "archer" in Latin. The constellation in the night sky is often depicted as having the appearance of a stick-figure archer drawing its bow.

The brighter stars in Sagittarius form an asterism known as The Teapot. The Milky Way is densest in Sagittarius, because the galactic center lies in that direction.

In astrology, Sagittarius is a fire sign. People born under it are said to be not superstitious. They are supposed to be drawn toward travel and philosophy, and to enjoy social contacts, meeting new people, and exploring other cultures. They are also said to be highly intelligent, visionary, and tolerant.

Sagittarians are considered compatible with Aries, Leo, and Gemini, and to a lesser extent with Taurus and Virgo.

Illustration by Edward Penfield

What Day of the Week is December 9?

On what day of the week does December 9 fall?

Surprisingly, this isn't an easy question. Because the calendar year is 365 days long (366 in leap years), it doesn't divide evenly by the seven days of the week.

Also, the Earth goes around the Sun in about 365-1/4 days, so a calendar tends to drift over time. That's why the same date falls on different weekdays in different years.

This is made even more complicated by a change in calendars that took place in 1582. Our modern calendar has its roots in ancient Rome, in a calendar reform conducted by Julius Caesar. Caesar commissioned mathematicians to attack the problem, and they came up with the idea of *leap years,* and thus standardized the calendar for centuries to come. This was called the *Julian calendar.*

Over time, however, the small errors in Caesar's calculation compounded. That's why Pope Gregory XIII commissioned the *Gregorian calendar,* used in most of the world today. Some countries converted in 1582, when the calendar was first developed;

some converted later; other still haven't changed.

Gregorian and Julian aren't the only types of calendars. The Hebrew year, the Islamic year, and many other calendars are used in different parts of the world and among different people.

You can convert Gregorian dates to other calendars, including the Hebrew calendar, the Islamic calendar, and even the Mayan calendar by visiting the Fourmilab Calendar Converter at http://www.fourmilab.ch/documents/calendar/.

Chinese calendar systems are quite complex and have changed several times; a full discussion is far beyond the scope of this book. If you're interested, you can find information here: http://www.hermetic.ch/cal_stud/chinese_cal.htm.

A 50-year brass perpetual calendar.

Copyright, Credit, and Contact

Follow Us

Our blog *Dobson's Improbable History* (http://improbhistory.blogspot.com) features short articles on events and people associated with each day, and updates several times each week. You can also get a daily "What Happened In History" message and all the latest Timespinner Press news by following us on Facebook at https://www.facebook.com/TimespinnerPress. Our Twitter feed @SidewiseThinker links you to all our News of the Day.

Contact Us

Find an error or a format problem? Want information about the series, about us, or about when the volume for your special day might be available? Please email us at editor@timespinnerpress.com. (We also take requests if your special day isn't yet complete. Please give us at least six weeks' notice if possible.)

On Dates

Historians use "CE" (Common Era) and "BCE" (Before the Common Era) instead of the more common "AD" (*Anno Domini*, or Year of Our Lord) and "BC" (Before Christ), reflecting the fact that the year-numbering system established by the Gregorian calendar is used throughout the world in many countries not culturally Christian.

The CE/BCE designation dates back to at least 1708, and has been adopted as a standard by the United Nations and the Universal Postal Union. Because this series of books covers events and people of all nations and cultures, we use the CE/BCE terms.

The abbreviation "O.S." ("Old Style") on some dates refers to the fact that the Russian Empire did not switch from the Julian to the Gregorian calendar at the same time as the rest of Europe, and therefore some figures and events have two dates. (See "What Day of the Week..." for an explanation of Julian and Gregorian dates.)

People and events whose original names are not in the Western alphabet have their native names (where possible) in the appropriate script shown in parenthesis. If you are using an e-reader to access an electronic version of this book, all characters don't always display on all devices.

Sources and Art Credits

We owe a great debt to Wikipedia, which is our first stop for research. We attempt to make independent confirmation of all important dates and facts through a variety of other sources. Other sources we frequently use include the Library of Congress; "on this day" listings from *Encyclopedia Britannica*, the New York *Times*, and the BBC; and, of course, the always essential Google.

All art and photographs are either in the public domain, used under a Creative Commons license, or with a "fair use" justification, and most frequently come from Wikimedia Commons and the Library of Congress Prints and Photographs Division.

Attribution is provided where requested by the copyright owner or when of historical significance, listed below. For information about any particular illustration or photograph, please contact us.

- The cover painting, "The Charge of the Light Brigade," is by Richard Caton Woodville, Jr., and was painted in 1894. It is in the public domain because its copyright has expired. The original is located in the Palacio Real de Madrid in Spain.

- The illustration of the month of December used on the back cover and as the frontispiece is from the 15th century French Gothic illuminated manuscript *Les Très Riches Heures du duc de Berry* by the Limbourg Brothers, Jean Colombe, and an intermediate painter whose name is lost to history. It is in the public domain because its copyright has expired.

- The photograph of Alfred, Lord Tennyson, was taken by Julia Margaret Cameron in 1869, and the original is in the collection of the Art Institute of Chicago. It is in the public domain because its copyright has expired.

- The first Christmas card was created by Sir Henry Cole in 1843, and is in the public domain because its copyright has expired.

- The 1752 painting of Saint Juan Diego witnessing the Virgin of Guadalupe is by Miguel Cabrera. It is in the public domain because its copyright has expired.

- The photograph of P. B. S. Pinchback was taken by either Mathew Brady or Levin Corbin Handy sometime between 1870 and 1800. It is in the public domain because its copyright has expired. The original image is part of the Brady-Handy Photograph Collection at the Library of Congress Prints and Photographs Division (LC-BH-826-3467).

- The photograph of Karl Brandt receiving the death sentence at the Nuremberg Doctor's Trial was taken in 1947, and is in the public domain as a work created by an employee of the US federal government. The original is part of the Telford Taylor Papers, Arthur W. Diamond Law Library, Columbia University Law School, New York, N.Y. : TTP-CLS: 15-1-1-76.

- The photograph of Petrified Forest National Park is by an employee of the National Park Service and is in the public domain as an image created by the US federal government.

- The image from the television program *A Charlie Brown Christmas* is covered by copyright and trademark of either the production company or the estate of creator Charles Schultz. It is used here under "fair use" provisions of US copyright law, to illustrate a historically significant event. No free or public domain alternatives exist, and the quality of the image is too low to allow the creation of counterfeit goods.

- The mug shot of Rod Blagojevich was taken by the US Marshals Service after Blagojevich's arrest. It is in the public domain as a work created by the US federal government.

- The 1978 photograph of Tip O'Neill was taken by a White House staff photographer and is in the public domain as a work created by the US government. The original is in the collection of the US National Archives and Records Administration (182078).

- The 1632 painting of Gustavus Adolphus of Sweden at the Battle of Breitenfeld is by Johann Walter, and can be found in the Musée historique de Strasbourg. The painting is in the public domain because its copyright has expired. The photograph of the painting was taken by "Rama," who has made it available under the terms of the French free software license CeCILL (http://www.cecill.info/licences/Licence_CeCILL_V2-en.html). The position of Timespinner Press is that a photograph of a public domain image is not itself an object of copyright. The image has been cropped for its use in this book.

- The 2007 photograph of Judi Dench at the BAFTA Awards was taken by Caroline Bonarde Ucci, and is used here under CC-BY-SA 3.0.

- The 1977 publicity photograph of Redd Foxx from *The Redd Foxx Show* is in the public domain because it was published in the US between 1923 and 1977 without a copyright notice.

- The 1950 publicity photograph of Kirk Douglas and Lauren Bacall from *Young Man With a Horn* is in the public domain because it was published in the US between 1923 and 1977 without a copyright notice.

- The publicity photograph of Margaret Hamilton and Judy Garland from the 1939 film *The Wizard of Oz* is in the public domain because it was published in the US between 1923 and 1977 without a copyright notice.

- The photograph of Emmett Kelly in a bubble bath was taken by Joseph Janney Steinmetz, a well known commercial photographer, as a favor to Kelly, who wanted the image for his Christmas card. The image is in the State Library and Archives of Flordia, and no known copyright restrictions exist on the use of this image.

- The publicity photograph from the television show *Amos 'n' Andy* was originally published in *Sponsor* magazine in 1952. Although there may or may not have been a copyright notice, the copyright was not renewed, and the work is therefore in the pubic domain.

- The photograph of Grace Hopper at the UNIVAC keyboard was taken around 1960, and is in the collection of the Smithsonian Institution (83-14878). It is used here under CC-BY-SA 2.0.

- The photograph of McKayla Maroney by White House staff photographer Pete Souza is cropped from a larger image taken with US President Barack Obama (P111512PS-0111) in the Oval Office in 2012. The image is in the public domain as a work created by the US federal government.

- The photograph "Star Players of the Baltimore Orioles" was taken around 1895. Although the work is in the public domain because its copyright is expired, it was uploaded by S. Dean Jameson, who has licensed it under CC-BY-SA 2.0. The original is in the McGreevey Collection at the Boston Public Library (06_06_000126).

- The 2010 photograph of Humayun Mirza is by Michael Dobson, and is used here under CC-BY-SA 3.0.

- The photograph of Dalton Trumbo at a 1947 session of the House Un-American Activities Committee is in the public domain as a work of the US government.

- The 1931 watercolor "Mariage et couronement du roi Babar et de la reine Céleste," *Histoire de Babar* ("Marriage and coronation of King Babar and Queen Celeste," *The Story of Babar*), is in the public domain in the European Union and non-EU countries with a copyright term of life of the author plus 70 years or less. The original is in the collection of The Morgan Library and Museum in Suffolk, Virginia.

- The painting of John Milton dictating *Paradise Lost* to his daughters was created circa 1826 by Eugène Delacroix. It is in the public domain because its copyright has expired.

- The self-portrait by Anthony van Dyck was painted sometime after 1633. It is in the public domain because its copyright has expired.

- The photograph of Douglas Corrigan is in the public domain as an image created by the US federal government.

- The photograph of Ralph Bunche at the 1963 March on Washington was taken for the Press and Publications Service (NWDNS-306-SSM-4D(63)9) and is used here under CC-BY-SA 2.0.

- The 1959 publicity photograph of Gene Barry was taken by NBC photographer Elmer Holloway. It is in the public domain because it was published in the US between 1923 and 1977 without a copyright notice.

- The poster for the 1927 film *Wings* is in the public domain because it was published in the US between 1923 and 1977 without a copyright notice.

- The 1956 publicity photograph of Bishop Fulton J. Sheen is in the public domain because it was published in the US between 1923 and 1977 without a copyright notice.

- The 1915 portrait of Edith Sitwell by Roger Fry is in the public domain because its copyright has expired.

- The 16th century oil on lapis lazuli painting *Perseus Rescuing Andromeda* is by Giuseppe Cesari. It is in the public domain because its copyright has expired. The original object is in the collection of the Saint Louis Art Museum.

- The 1882 painting of *Ilex aquifolium* (holly) is by Anton Hartinger, and appeared originally in the book Atlas der Alpenflora.

- The artist who created the 18th century painting of a Hannukah celebration is unknown. The painting is in the public domain because its copyright has expired.

- The 1660 drawing of the heavens is by Johannes van Loon, and was first published in *Harmonia Macrocosmica* by Andreas Cellarius. It is in the public domain because its copyright has expired.

- The photograph of the 1906 automobile calendar by Edward Penfield is from the Library of Congress Prints and Photographs Division, and is in the public domain because it was published prior to January 1, 1923.

- The 50-year perpetual calendar photograph is in the public domain.

- The painting on the last page, *Labors of the Month: December*, by Simon Bening, was published in a Flemish Book of Hours in the first half of the 16th century. It is in the public domain because its copyright has expired.

License Description and Terms

Aside from material purely in the public domain, photographs and other material in this book are used under specific licenses permitting free use, usually with attribution. For full text and terms of these licenses, click or enter the appropriate links below.

- Creative Commons Attribution 2.0 Generic (CC-BY 2.0): http://creativecommons.org/licenses/by/2.0/deed.en

- Creative Commons Attribution-Share Alike 3.0 Generic (CC-BY-SA 3.0): http://creativecommons.org/licenses/by-sa/3.0/

- Creative Commons Attribution-Share Alike 2.5 Generic (CC-BY-SA 2.5): http://creativecommons.org/licenses/by-sa/2.5/deed.en

- Creative Commons Attribution-Share Alike 2.0 Generic (CC-BY-SA 2.0): http://creativecommons.org/licenses/by/2.0/deed.en http://creativecommons.org/publicdomain/zero/1.0/deed.en

- Creative Commons Attribution-Share Alike 1.0 Generic (CC-BY-SA 1.0): http://creativecommons.org/licenses/by-sa/1.0/deed.en

- CC0 1.0 Universal (CC0 1.0) Public Domain Dedication (CC0 1.0)

- GNU Free Documentation License (GFDL): http://en.wikipedia.org/wiki/Wikipedia:Text_of_the_GNU_Free_Documentation_License

Labors of the Month: December, by Simon Bening